AF220354

TURTLES & PAPERCLIPS

Poems

Volume II

2022

Production and publishing: BoD – Books on Demand,
Norderstedt
ISBN: 9783756275328

ABOUT THE AUTHOR

Born in Neustrelitz, Germany on December 14, 1998 Alena began her studies of English Literature + Culture and English Linguistics at Paderborn University at 19. Writing has proven the best therapy to help her through the difficulties and painful things in life. She first tried a hand at poetry in late 2018.

Other Publications:
Turtles & Paperclips – Ironies in Writing (2022)

Find her on...
Instagram: alenarehse
Pinterest: alenarehse
Twitter: alena_rehse

Forgive me for not speaking up sooner—
Writing´s all I know how to do

100 poems

Sections

This is all about <u>you</u> this time anyway

Scan to find the TURTLES Playlist on Spotify

4

I get this funny feeling that
Writing about you
Only made it worse

So,
So much worse

But it was the only way I had
To find relief
From the burden of my feelings

This is my confessional
My deepest apology

Yes,
The one you never wanted to hear

I

Hoping

How can blue eyes
Spread such warmth?
How can they make me
Feel so at home?

Believe in You

I tried to tell you
That I believe in you

And I wonder:

Do you see the same in me
That I have long since seen in you?

I love you and I
Don't think that'll ever change

Cause whatever they see in me
Is everything I'll never be

But when you take one look at me
I see everything I wanna be

You should know:

If there is one thing that is true
It's that I believe in you

Our Poughkeepsie

Sorry for sharing
What was supposed to be
And stay between us;
It made for such a fitting metaphor.

But maybe you´re right and
Nobody gets it anyway.
What it really stands for
Only we will know.

And if I am honest
I don´t care anymore
If the world takes notice.
This will always be
Our Poughkeepsie.

Only One

I like that we can talk
The way that we do.

When it comes to
Things like this
You´re the only one
I want to talk to.

Here or in London

In all this mess
There is one thing I am sure of

I´ll be your friend
And you´ll be mine

Whether here
Or in London

Special to Me

Only man I ever
Shared a bed with
For no other reason
Than sleeping;
Whose place I spent the night at

Only one I ever
Shared my deepest
And darkest secrets with
Only reason I am here today

The one whom I have
Written about enough
To fill a whole book

Don´t ever tell me again
That you are not special

You´re special to me

Hawkeye Said

"It doesn't happen too often, but
Every once in a while,
You come across somebody
That just makes you better in every way"

That's what Hawkeye said.
And I immediately thought of you.

Not the Only Dreamer

No matter what I tell you
I´m not smart
When it comes to making plans
Or realistic expectations
I always aim to high
And fall too far
Countless times I´ve proven this
It´s the thought I wake up to:
Learning from mistakes
Is something I don´t do

In matters of the heart
Love, and faith, and family
You´re a naïve and
Silly little boy sometimes
Who´d put Peter Pan to shame
People are a vicious species
Never quite so good at heart
As you make them to be

It seems to me quite obvious
I´m not the only one who´s crazy
Who believes in things irrational
Not the only dreamer

Wait 4 You

If it only happens
By the end of the year
Or when we´re 30
Then that´s fine
I´d wait my whole life for you

Just the Possibility

it was hard not to read a maybe
in your words
between the lines
not to keep a little hope alive
with just the possibility
in reach

right there
at my fingertips

or so it seemed

May 20th

Drunk enough to kiss you once again
But we are not alone now
I´m sure I wouldn´t do it anyway
Too shy for one
And it wouldn´t be adequate
It wouldn´t be what we need
But what I want is
Something else yet
It´s you, right now
Your lips, your touch
And your heart while we´re at it
All of you
And there is one thing I am willing to give for it:
All of me

That´s the deal
That I have to offer

Can we do that please?

I Hope for You

I hope
You´ll never know
The pain that I knew
Because of you

I Will

If there is absolutism in love
       You´re my definition
My best and worst experience
       Of everything my heart is
       Capable of feeling
The peak of what I can take
       And every dream I´m hoping for
       When I go to sleep
In you I found a will to live
       And the hardest pain I can endure

I will love you to the end of time
       If you allow it
I´ll spend my life with you
       If you let me
I will wait forever
       If that´s how long it takes
For you to fall for me, too

II

Drowning

You know all the things about me
I would never admit in daylight
Cause late night talking's how we do

Just So You Know

Just so you know:
I won´t be texting you anymore.
I´ll just wait for you,
Like I will always wait for you.
But the rejection is growing more painful
And I cannot handle the disappointment anymore.

I love you.
Just so you know…

Her

I still feel like dying
Every time you say her name
Every fucking time you mention her

My Foolish Heart

People often notice
I´m no savourer
I´m just a drinker

Am no smart mind either
Lose myself in hopeless dreaming
Instead of doing some reflecting

So I couldn´t know that
It would be this hard
Don´t blame my foolish heart

Expectations

You fulfil so many expectations
I didn´t even know I had
Which only leads to new ones rising
That you cannot help but disappoint

Why Aren´t You?

You are probably unsure
Whether there can be more
After so much time
When there wasn´t.
I don´t know that either.
But I am willing
To find out.
Why, oh why aren´t you?

Being Your Friend

Being your friend
Is so incredibly exhausting
It's so damn hard
Someone needed to tell you that

Deal with It

Do you think this is a joke?
Do you think I'm over you?

You still don't know
How to deal with it, do you?
With those feelings that I have.
I thought you'd have gotten used to it by now.

Walking Home

He is complaining
About the cold
And the long way.
Makes me think of the countless times
You walked me home
And the funny conversations
That we had.

Chose the Pain

I chose the pain of the Maybe
Over the pain of a No
And that is not your fault
It's mine

Not with You Around

Me and some friends, we
Got high on the rooftops last night
And I thought of you and I
Couldn´t get there
When you were with me
Could never do it
And feel this good
When you were around

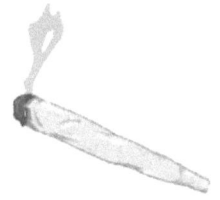

On My Mind

The thought of you
Still makes me cry sometimes
Like just now without a warning
Tears come running out my eyes
I´m still drifting on the afterglow
Have lost count of
How many went around
But that stuff was good, I tell you
I´m riding on that late bus now
Homewards, brain still foggy and slow
And you like always on my mind

My Sad Goodbye

Being drunk, it´s
The best medicine
For a broken heart

Trying to ignore
The sound of you over there
I´m just sitting here
And compose my sad goodbye

It´s so hard to stay away from you
It´s so hard to stay sober
When I´m near you

Guess I´ll just stay drunk forever
And end my misery
The day that you
Fall in love with another

Can´t Fight

I can´t fight with you
All you have to say´s one thing
And I am so damn sorry
For everything I ever did
Everything I am

May 8th

We´re out again
Drinking in daytime now
But there are too many other people around
I´m getting claustrophobic again
They trigger my anxiety

You ask me for a cigarette
But it´s for that girl you´re with
I hold out the lighter
Even before you realise
You don´t got one

You light that cigarette for her
And when you hand it back
You say "Thank You"
In a tone that makes me hope
You see how fucked-up this is

For me

The Terminology

I´m still thinking it
Every time I look at you
No matter whether
You´re talking to me or not

Cannot say what I really wanna say
Have only known it myself
Since we talked about the terminology

Before that,
Trust me, I have had these thoughts
But only for a second
I´ve allowed them
To then push them far away
And avoid rethinking them
Ever

Until it happened

Nearly Over You

I´m staring into
That candle fire
Listening to
Adele singing
About the pain I´m feeling
Now I´m nearly over you
Yeah, that´s
What I´m telling myself, too

Talk

If you ever do want to talk about it
Give me a heads-up, please
Odds are I won´t yet be
Quite drunk enough
For that conversation
Give me 20 minutes or so
Then we can talk

Salt Water

Craving you´s like
Drinking salt water

The River

In my land of memories
I will
Name a river after you
It´ll be so lovely, playful
And peaceful like you
And I´ll never be able to hold it
Always flowing away
Running through my fingertips

Pretend

I can´t forget you
But I can pretend
That we´re fine
And when the lights are out
I´ll cry for a bit
Then keep going
The next morning

I can put on an act
Until I don´t have to pretend anymore

Closer

I want to be closer
But I´m still not sure
If that wouldn´t make it
Even harder

All the Time

I´m used to looking at things I want
But cannot have.

I look at you all the time.

Staying Over

And I still sometimes stay over
Even though I know
That really doesn´t make it better

Your Things in My Apartment

I got that chair in my kitchen
That used to be
On your balcony
I got that old clock on the wall
That used to belong
To your old flatmate

And my coffee table;
I remember how
You built that for me
The cabinet I use
To store my food—
That used to be your dresser

And the other clock,
The one in my room,
It used to be in yours;
Stuck around 11
For as long as I´ve known you
But I changed the batteries
When you gave it to me
And when you were here
You checked the time on your phone
Cause you weren´t used to
That clock working right

How the fuck am I supposed to
Not think about you
When my world runs over with you

32

Something I Shouldn't Do

Right now I am
Drunk enough to kiss you
I'd do it, for real
Just like that
And it's so definitely
Something I shouldn't do

Another Notch on My Belt

The passions of
The night before
Just another
Notch on my belt

Never spend the night though
I got my principles, too
But really I don't wanna
Get used to another

What if believing in the Maybe
Is what kept me going all this time?
And now that I've accepted
The truth of the No
I'll stumble and break down?

33

Sorry

I´m sorry
I gotta say it
Even if it´s the one thing you don´t wanna hear
Even if it´s the last thing I´ll ever say to you
Oh God, I hope it´s not

You gotta know
That sabotaging what we had
Was the last thing on my mind
You can´t imagine
What our friendship means to me

Yes, I love you
And I guess I always will
But please, oh God, please don´t ever
Let that get in the way of
What we have now
It will always mean so much more

There´s a book about finding
Someone who can break and heal your heart
Written by me
And my big bag of regrets

Happy

I love him
That's the one thing I am sure of
The only thing I'll ever know is true

You don't answer and
I take all these things so personally
Knowing they are not

Desperate for you to need me
Angry at the world
For not giving me the ability
To make you happy

I wish I could give you
The kind of love that you deserve
But I can't
Not with a body this weak
Or a mind this broken

I will live my life and try
To do what you wished me I would
But I'll always, always think of you, my friend

I can see it happen already
Over a thousand corners I'll have heard
That you settled down
And that you're happy

Despairing

Don't care about my stupid heart
It's good for nothing
Except loving you

The Distance

Live in the same town
Yet I am missing you

Only one call away
Whether night or day

Still I feel the distance
Like a constant vibration

Which won´t let me rest
Or choose happiness instead

But

I love you, but
In a manner that
Doesn´t allow for romance
Even if that was
An actual option

And that drives me crazy

Attention

Fighting for your attention
When I have been fighting for
So much already
Is draining

My strength to persevere,
My patience,
And will to keep going;
My absolutely everything

It´s draining me
Yet I am so painfully aware
I have no right
No right at all
To ask of you
What I am craving
More than anything

I´m craving you

Falling Apart

I´m going to bed
But not with you

Try to sleep
And think of you

When alone I´m okay
All well and good, except

I´m falling apart
Without you

My Secrets

I left
The furthest reaches of my comfort zone
The moment
I told you my first secret

And by now you
Know so fucking many
Nobody can tell me
This shit ain´t scary

Late in November

The uncertainty that´s
Driving me mad
Is not the only reason
For my constant hesitation
There´s also that hopelessness
In the vision of you and me
While knowing that
I´d rather have this with you
Than nothing at all

Almost

And again I´m staring
At the open chat on the screen
I almost typed "I love you" this time

Trying

I´m trying so desperately
To learn
How to keep being friends with you
And simultaneously
Keep my feelings alive
Only just in case
You do come around one day

The second thing, it
Actually takes no work at all
Years from now
I´ll still want you
Like the first day

But that first bit
Gives me trouble
I need you way too much
In that friend way
And like you far too much
To still introduce you
As my best friend
And not flinch at the words

That is something you will always be to me, no problem
But why can´t you be something else as well?

A Little Piece of Me

Don´t care
About their attention anymore
I only care about yours

Every time you interrupt me
When I´m in the middle of a sentence
A little piece of me dies

I go out for no reason at all
My feet carry me
To your bar
So automatically

You tell me to
Turn to you when I need to
But when I do, it seems that you
Don´t take it seriously at all

But I think we both know
I will always forgive you
No matter how much it breaks me

You could ignore and shatter me
And a little piece of me
Would always want you

Friend Like You

It´s funny, but I
Never knew a man like you;
Never found love to be
A thing worth living for.

It´s sad, but I
Never had a friend like you;
Never knew depression
Before I fell in love this hard.

What do I have to do
To make you love me,
Make you see me
The way that I see you?

Trust me with your secrets,
But never with your heart;
Don´t you believe that I would
Guard it just the same?

I will never forget
Looking into those eyes
While you guessed all the things
That I just couldn´t say.

I´m trying again
Before my voice breaks
Because I know
Silence never suited you.

I will never forget
Standing there with you
In the lamplight late at night
Talking around the bush.

I´m failing again
It´s only been my millionth try;
And I keep thinking
That´s not what you deserve.

You got some history, and
I thought I´d been in love before,
But then you came along
Teaching me that I was wrong.

Too much for every day, but
When you leave
You´ll be gone again,
And that´s what my heart can´t take…

It´s so easy to fall for you;
So hard to love you.

Deathly

I am sorry I fell in love with you
And brought all these things to our friendship
That you didn´t like
Believe me, neither did I

I´m afraid that
By doing what I did
I broke some things
I never should have touched

I want you to want me
The way I want you
I need you to need me
The way I need you

Without boundaries
Desperately
Woeful
Deathly

Because of You

I get jealous for no reason
Possessive of someone
I have no right to love

Wait, that's wrong
I have every right
Just still don't feel worthy
Of ~~someone like~~ you

Make un-called-for accusations
Who even am I
To criticise a man like you?

I've become everything
I never wanted to be
And it's all because of you

Friend Zone

God, I hate this friend zone
It's an awful place to
Spend a million years in

Lily & Snape

If I ever stumble upon
A kid with her hair
And your eyes
I swear it will kill me

You are the Lily of my story
I am your Severus

In the morning I can´t help
But be mad at you
Don´t you see how serious
It could have been?
How much it troubled me
Not to know?
Do you still doubt my feelings for you?

Want You

Drifting through space again
Got me thinking
Of what it would feel like
Losing myself in the passion with you
What it would be like
Having you in this bed with me
Don´t get me wrong, I´ve had these thoughts before
But it´s never been this vivid in my head
Can almost feel you on my skin now

I want you

Have never said that
To anyone

Never Leave Me

Another one of those one-night-stands
It's getting harder to keep up
Counting's never been a strength of mine

You do know you're the reason, do you?
One of them, for sure
And maybe you will gladly hear
That the whole thing has
Fulfilled its purpose
In giving me some self-esteem
After the rejections of the past

But the empty spot residing in my heart
That I have tried to fill, it's
Only emptier than ever
Cause you feel farther than before
A stranger to my heart
Kin of my lonely soul

You'll never leave me, will you?

March 3ʳᵈ

I still love you way too much
Don´t know if I can ever stop

Bruised and battered and alone
In bed, licking my wounds

Wondering if they can ever heal
The pain tells me it was true

And I´m asking the ceiling:
Can there be love after you?

March 21ˢᵗ

Give me just
A little bit of your love
That could make me
The happiest I´ve ever been
Just to be someone
Worthy of your affection

See, I hold you
In such high esteem
And maybe that´s just me
But maybe you can find it in yourself
To deem it relevant
My pathetic admiration

No Excuse

I even moved
Closer to your place
What the hell was I thinking
Now I got no excuse anymore
To stay over
No, I don´t
Except laziness, you offered
And maybe the fact that you said that
Means
That you still want me to
That having me sleep next to you
Is really not that bad at all
Have we gotten used to each other
In this complicated way?
Why, oh, how could we…
I fell in love with you
Laying in that bed
Staring at your back
Listening
To your breathing
Deep and heavy
Loaded with the burdens that you carry
Needing the relief that is offered
By sleep alone
I can´t give that to you
But, oh, my dear, I want to
Give you the worldß

April 23rd

I can´t say I love you
Because you don´t wanna hear it
Said you couldn´t handle it

I can´t write you letters anymore
Cause you told me what that does to you
Cannot consciously put that on you

Hear you breathing behind me
Fall asleep to the reverie
Of a simpler life
With nothing to come between you and I

Anything

The worst thing is
I´d still do anything
That you´d want me to
No questions asked
I´d do anything
Just to spend
A little time with you
I´d choose you
Over anything else
Anything, I´d do it
Anything for you

All That We Will Ever Be

You finally realised
How serious it really is
And reacted in a way
That I didn´t foresee

Is this the only way I get to take you home with me?
Is this all that we will ever be?

Again I wonder why
You only ever show that sort of interest
When it gets serious like this

I am grateful for your friendship
Disappointed in your indifference
Know that´s not what it is
But dream about what it could be instead

In love so deeply
And unrequitedly
It drives me crazy

But then I get that hope back
And I´m fine again
Isn´t that unhealthy?

A circle I can´t break out of
Until the day you tell me
You finally return my feelings

Today for the first time
I had another thought
What if we aren't as unbreakable
As we thought we were?

What if holding onto this friendship
Wasn't the best thing we could do?

It's a scary idea but
After a day not talking
I get the feeling that it's possible
For me to live without you

In that case we
Might be strangers
And there'll be nothing left but

Turtles
And West Highland Terriers

May 24th

I want to be someone you can love
But, guess what, I can´t
Not with all the therapy in the world
And I am facing the tragic truth:
I´d rather die than not be with you

The Other Side

Now I think I´ll never know
What tenderness feels like
What love is truly like
I´ll only ever know
What I know now
Cause you wouldn´t show me
The other side

Every Time I Stay Over

We were walking home
Drunk together, yet again
It was too late for me to get a bus
And you too good to let me go alone

I sank crying to the ground
With the heaviness of my thoughts
You said I was the one who
Knew most of your secrets

And I am flattered, but
Being a confident of your heart
Does not change anything
About my physical desire

And it gets stronger
Every time I stay over

Love

Love can be
A taste so sweet
Like strawberries
On Belgium chocolate

Love starts in the heart
And moves to the body from there
Passions of the soul
Bring with them
The physical desire

What can I say,
You are no Jensen Ackles,
Somerhalder or DiCaprio
But I want you more
Than I could ever want
Any of them

Love can be
A feeling so strong
Like a migraine
Or radiation poisoning

Others have survived love
Why, oh why can´t I?

IV

Saving

I never wanted to lose you
But I think I held on too long

You Changed Me

Falling for you
Was unavoidable
I see that now

I really wish we would have met
Just a little later
When we both would have been ready

Falling for you
Did me good
I swear it did

You changed my attitude
My patronus
And my life

You changed me

Cibola

Started out so simple
And now there´s

Only chaos between me and you
A festival of fools

I believe that this is us
And this is ours

And in that chaos we will find
Our city of gold

Others

With other men to focus on
I don´t feel that bad anymore
Because of you

I can accept both our feelings
And find relief in
What *they* can give me

Maybe This is What I Owe You

I have tried my best
Yet it has always lead me
To my very worst

Countless times I decided to grind on
Even though I knew, deep in my heart,
It would never be worth it
In the end

With the world at the brim of catastrophe
And my means not covering for my dreams
Tell me what´s the reason
To keep living?

Ever since we started being friends
You told me you´d be there any time of day
And lived up to your promise
Even if I didn´t always see it that way

I told the world you were the only reason
And I do believe I meant it
Maybe I´d still be here without ever knowing you
But I´d be off a lot worse than I am now

My suffering has not yet ended
And my belief in myself, well, it
Has only flared up shortly
I´ve lost touch again
With that special part of me

The future's looking dark now
Nothing there that fits me
Nothing in this world worth living for
Living
Just isn't for me

And as I'm making plans
For how to spend the end
I'm reminded of the person who
Has always given me
What no one else ever could or wanted to

It overwhelmed me at times
As you well know
I simply wasn't used to it
Didn't know how to give back
Struggled with not needing to

Just today you told me again
Things will solve themselves somehow
You're clearly crazy
Best friend I'll ever have
Best person I will ever know
Constant inspiration
Hopeless optimist

And if you want me to keep fighting
Well, then I guess I probably should

After everything
Maybe this is what I owe you

Our Friendship

Yesterday
I tried to be there for *you* for a change
But you wouldn´t let me
I´m not sure how to feel comfortable in a friendship
Where you only ever give, and never take

I have decided to not write you any letters anymore
You may have noticed
I want to say what I want you to know
And what I cannot say,
Well, those are the things you shouldn´t hear

And probably shouldn´t know

PS:

I have been thinking
About us
And I believe I have
Reached a conclusion now

As long as you want this
I want it too

Lifeline

Accepting what you said
Back in December
As the "No" it should have been
Is what finally helped me
Getting better

I clung to the "Maybe"
For too long
Did it out of desperation
Seized it like a lifeline
And simply forgot to stop
When the danger was over

But luckily
That is now behind me
Let´s have fun again
The way we used to

Find the Way

Gotta find my way now
To a new and better me
You´re gonna find your way now
That you don´t have to worry about me

Up 2 You

Not getting to see you
Hurts me more, so much more
Than spending time with you does

So my decision´s made
The rest
Is up to you

For Real This Time

I´m using you
As a lifeline
Once again
But it´s about
Life and death
This time
You can´t carry
All my baggage on your own, though
I promise you I´ll find another
And I´m ready
Ready for another lifeline
For real
This time

March 18th

You hurt me more than any other person
Ever did or could
But you only have that kind of power
Because you mean so much more to me
And I care about you truly
And maybe that is why I´m stayin´

Right now I am thinking those thoughts
Sitting outside your bar
Counting the cigarettes until you´re back

And Then There's You...

Do not wonder 'bout my strange behaviour
That's just how my mind works
It's what they call madness

Looking for order
In a world that doesn't know it
Stranger to the concept

When people laugh in my vicinity
I always wonder
Is it about me?

And then there's you
Somebody as good as no one
That I ever knew

A day I didn't speak with you
Is a day lost
In my memory it won't exist

A beacon in the night
You're there when no one else is
I didn't know it was you I miss

Do not love me now, or ever
But in the end
You make life hurt less
You always make it better

To the End

When will I be bold enough
To call us kindred souls
And find the self-esteem
To compare myself to you
In that way

But it is quite clear, now, isn´t it?
We´re the same
In our pain and what it made us
Kindred spirits
To the end

V

A Little Bit of All of It

And if forever's what it takes
I'll bide my time
And love you when I can
But then I'll do it fiercely
Unredeemable

"Hey"

I went back in our chat
All the way to the top
I saw that I was wrong
When I said that photo you sent me
Was how it started
No, turns out we texted
A short while before
We said "hey"
A "hey" was how we started
A "hey" was my doom

I Remember

I remember
Coming to your door
That very first day
Nervous to
Begin something new

I remember
Being in your room
For the very first time
How could I not know then
I was on a direct way to fall in love
Maybe ´cause I never knew what that was

I remember
Every movie night I came over for
Cause there was nothing else for us to do
Outside, the world was on hold
Inside, we became friends
Neither had others in this town
So was it unavoidable?

71

I remember
How annoyed I was
By your constant talking
Nasty habits, and loud noises
And how I thought, every time
This might be the last time
But I still came back
Every Wednesday

I remember
Being in your room
For the very last time
All empty, except for memory
The day that you moved
It was the same day I realised
What you had done to me
Without ever meaning to
And I was lost

I remember the people we were a year ago
I hope that
I will always remember

Better than You

I´m slowly accepting that
You´re not what I need

But oh, you came so close
I doubt that a person exists

Who can do better than that
And still be real

Cause who can possibly
Be better than you?

And if I can´t have you, I know
I won´t ever do better

There´s no better than you

Kick Something

I just need to kick something
When it gets too much
Same way you need to punch a wall
We´re both a little messed-up, aren´t we?

Spill a Secret by Mistake

I write so much about you
Makes me worry that sometime by mistake
I´ll spill a secret
You would rather keep

Could Be Good

How can I offer you
A heart as weak as mine
How could I think
It would be enough

Even if I´m nothing to you
You´re fucking everything to me
Isn´t this unhealthy?

I know I´m a difficult friend
No idea how you´ve been doing it
But I swear if you can deal with it a little longer
I will be good for you

Knowledge is responsibility, you say
I hate to have put that on you
In a world that breaks us
Makes us unbelievers
And puts our character to test

I think I can be good for you

With a heart a little less weak
And a past not quite so messed-up
With a steady mind

I´m sure I could be good for you

I hope you´re aware
I´d drop it all in a second
If you changed your mind
And loved me tomorrow

Why does everybody say it´s wrong
To fixate on one person
If he´s the only one who´s good for me?

It´s come to the point where
It´s either being loved by you
Or dying

I don´t see any other way
Don´t want new friends
I just want you

I can´t deal with changing tides
Or the passing of time
You´re the only constant I´m aware of

Jealousy is
Driving me mad
Never thought
It could be like that

If we will be this
Or we´ll be more
In any case I´ll try

I´ll try to be good for you

I Still Wonder About You

I still wonder sometimes
About you
About how cool you are with it
How you can detach yourself
And view things objectively
Even though you know so well
Every word is in reality
About you alone
Inspired by your words
And everything you did
Still it doesn't faze you much
Sometimes I wonder about you

Loving You

I thought it's easy
To love something beautiful
It's not easy—loving you
You're pure, yet deadly so
Too flawed to speak of perfection
And still too good to be true
A do-gooder by profession
Exhausting as nothing
Yet I think the world of you

Me and the People I´ve Lost

My body´s covered in
Tattoos about
Me and the people I´ve lost

A collection to which
I never want to add
A tattoo about you

Sleep

I cannot sleep
If you and I aren´t good
That´s the reason I keep texting you
Even though we both are tired
And you have just been here anyway
I will keep texting
Until I feel better
About the things between us
And if I don´t do that
That´s a conscious choice
Cause at least one of us
Deserves the peace that only sleep can offer

In Love Quietly

I´m sorry the whole world took notice
Of what went on between you and me
I just can´t
Be in love quietly
It´s too exciting

The Night

This is the night that I´ll remember
As the night the decision was made
Been a long time since December
Not enough to heal, but
Plenty to realise
What you were really telling me
Is that it´s been hopeless all along
Even if you didn´t know that at the time

Before I Go

I want to taste love
With my own lips
Will I ever be allowed to
Make that experience
Before I go?

  I know if I am
  My kiss will say
  We could have had something beautiful
  But our time's over now
  And I dare say
  That despite everything
  That we missed out on
  We did use it well

    I'm not wondering anymore
    How long I'll love you
    The answer is in every thought of you

      I hate it
      When things are over
      That you wish had
      Gone on forever

Friends

You and me together
Is that thought really so odd to you?
We spend all our time together anyway
Text every single day
And confide in each other
All the secrets no one else gets to hear

Do you remember
All the moments that
Our friendship's made of
The way that I do?
I'm sitting in the rain alone
Smoking and writing once again
Waiting silently for your reply
Hoping that today's a day I get to see you
Still wondering
Do friends feel the way that I do?

I used to be stronger
Now I am only
Craving their pity
And that's when it hit me

I stopped thinking only about myself
When you and I met
Wanted to help, and
Ignored what I needed
Just for you
Is that what friends do?

A good friend…
Is that still what I am to you?

All of my friends think
What we have is toxic
When before they could have sworn
You liked me too

From their point of view
It could have all been puppies and rainbows
Between me and you
Summer rain in May

All of my friends say
We'd make a great fit
But the way that I see it
We're good together
Like June and December

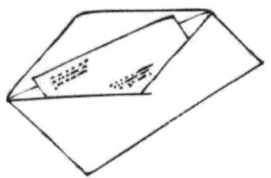

Never so Bold

That last letter, it
Was pretty daring, wasn´t it?
I re-read it
Last time I was at your place and
Found it on the counter

I am never so bold
Or brave
As when I write
Can you even call something brave
That comes to you so easily?

Hear It from Me

I love you

I kind of really wanted you
To hear that from me
Instead of reading it between the lines
Of random poems

Hey you,

There´s a few things I wanna say
And even though I speak to you daily
I cannot seem to find the right time

I have always been able
To be straight with you
Talk honestly and open
About my feelings
Whatever they may be
And yet I still find it difficult
To broach certain topics
My love for you is one
My frustration yet another

You know, from this experience,
What love means to me?

It means that I suffer
When you suffer
Every time, and I am powerless
Can´t change the situation
Cannot be there for you
Cause you never let me

It means I get annoyed over-quickly,
Everything that you do, it fucks me up
In a thousand facets
And I am powerless, once again

It means I see you happy
And I´m torn
Cause I rarely see you happy anymore
When you´re with me

It hurts me
When you hurt yourself
It kills me
When you talk of dying

Seven letters I have written you
You let me wait for answers
Every time
After that fight, that one night
I swore not to write another
Talking is the better way
But, darling, it´s been difficult
And I feel I need to write you
Just a couple more

And this one has been
A long time coming

I want you to know
You made a better person out of me
Made me something
I never thought I could be

I never thought I could be good
But I am a little better
Did it for you

I never knew that
I could love this hard
It hurts
Like no pain I ever knew
And I´ve known plenty
This you can believe me

I felt alone with this pain
But not alone
Cause you were there for me still
Even when it was you
Who caused the problem

I told my mother about you…

I am sorry
That you couldn´t love me back
You missed out on something big

As you are going through life
Just be aware
No one will ever
Love you like I do

And, by the way,
If you never want to be with me
You should probably
Not let me wear your jacket again
I like the smell far too much

Punching Walls

Guess what, I´m punching walls now, too
Always with my left hand
I need the other one to write
But, oh, I understand now
It hurts like hell
But the pain is welcome
Annoying for a while
And then
Strangely satisfying

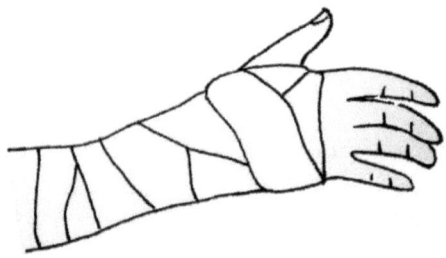

July 11th

A minute before his birthday
You had to tell me
You almost had a date
With another

And that it was months ago
You thought you were ready
Now you know you're not
But back then
You didn't choose me

I know I was a mess
But why, oh why
Did you have to do that
To my fragile heart

Still so fragile...

You know this girl
She offered you her heart
Said to you
All the things she never says
And you went along
Made her your friend
Closer than most
Distant like no one
And if you can't love her back
At least be mindful
Of how you treat her
Every word you say to her
Watch out
With a girl so fragile
A person this damaged
A human so weak
A hundred times hurt before
And yet there's
This little bit of love
Left in her heart
And she reserved it

...For You

The heavy irony
Between you and me
I cannot help myself
It's kind of funny

100 poems
About you and me
100 poems
For the world to see

Have been writing this for ages
I'm thinking maybe
It's too much misery
For 80 pages

A bunch of poems
Short and long
But all of them
Made of love and pain

100 poems
To try and make you see
100 poems
About something

That we may never be

You'll never love me,
will you?

Fun fact:
The word "you" occurs a total of 440 times in this book